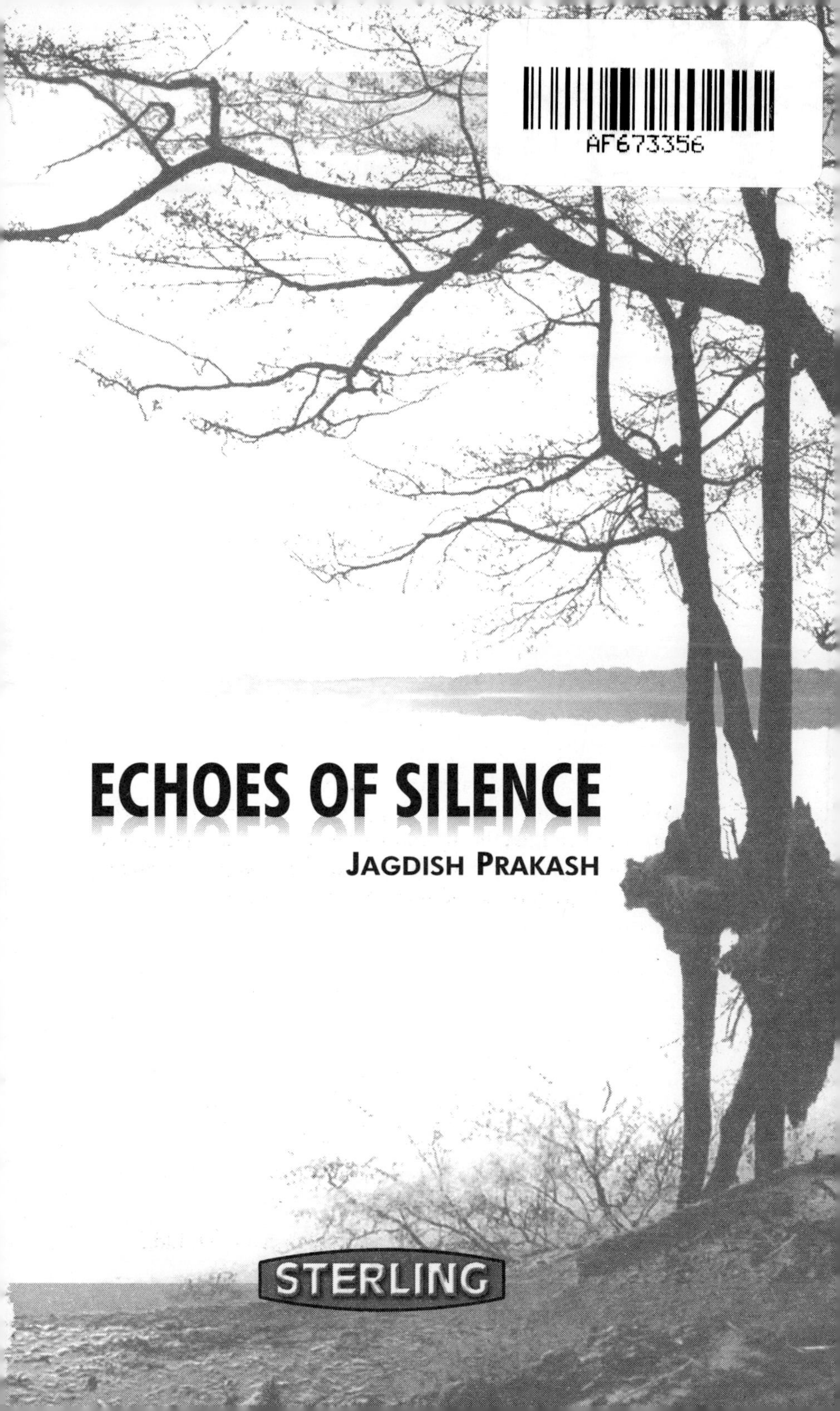

ECHOES OF SILENCE

JAGDISH PRAKASH

STERLING

STERLING PAPERBACKS
An imprint of
Sterling Publishers (P) Ltd.
A-59, Okhla Industrial Area, Phase-II,
New Delhi-110020.
Tel: 26387070, 26386209; Fax: 91-11-26383788
E-mail: mail@sterlingpublishers.com
www.sterlingpublishers.com

Echoes of Silence

ISBN 978 81 207 6885 7

Printed in India

Printed and Published by Sterling Publishers Pvt. Ltd.,
New Delhi-110 020.

Dedicated to

Those silent moments
Which become poems.

Poetry is an orphan of silence.
The words never quite equal
the experience behind them.

— *Charles Simic*

The Echo of My Silence

'Poetry is an echo asking for a shadow to dance.'

—Carl Sandburg

'Echoes of Silence' is the first collection of my poems in English. These poems have been written at different times, under different moods, under the impact of different situations and, hence, are reflective of different streams of thought and subjects.

Both Urdu and English languages are the thought vehicles of my emotional content. As such, an overlap of influence of one language over the other is natural and inevitable. Writing poetry is not my profession, nor is it my everyday routine. But beyond the clichéd existential reality lies another reality, the reality of perceptions, feelings, memories, emotions, unrequited wishes, delights, frustrations, etcetera which get their tempering from everyday experiences. I hear the soliloquies of this inner reality, this surreal happening, reverberating in the antechamber of my inner silences. These silences, when they overflow, express themselves in myriad echoes which sprout into poems. My poems, therefore, are less a narration of events, situations or manifest happenings; they allude to events, situations or happenings merely as contextual props for expression of the impact which these experiences cast on emotions. In the words of T S Eliot, "Poetry...is not the expression of personality, but an escape from personality...."

My poems, too, are my attempts to escape from the events I order to fathom into the post-happening impact of the event. They are emotional statements of a felt reality.

I am not concerned here so much with the correctness of syntax or form, or the appropriate usage of words or idioms in these poems. As I said earlier, my Urdu expressions, thought streams and phrasing might have a bearing upon my English expressions as well. I do not claim any degree of sufficiency of expression in English language as I have never had the privilege to learn English in an English language classroom in an elite public school. My focus is more on expressing my feelings with the same intensity with which I have experienced them at an emotional level.

I wish you, the reader, to be my fellow traveler on my journey through the undefined territory of my inner reality. It is possible you may find a convergence of your own path in it.

Jagdish Prakash

Contents

Today

I am lost to myself
The way memories are lost to time,
The rain to a parched earth,
The song to the silence of a grave.

I don't know where one stays in
The dorm of sentiments;
The ladder in the attic of desires slips suddenly
And the concrete crumbles the bricklay base.

Where do I go from here?

The city mourns, the roads shriek,
A sudden downpour washes the last traces of
All that I cherished one cool morning
Long long ago.

A Morning sans Morning

No smiles, no words,
No gestures, no conjectures.
Devoid of formalities,
Morning emerges
Sparkling from anonymity, yet
Ruthlessly strange and introvert.

The shimmering rays
Touch the window sill
But stand still,
Waiting for something to happen,
Something to be said, explained.
Slowly the moments dissolve
Into alleys of ashen apparitions,
An orchestra of noises rehearses
As hordes converge in streets,
Markets, bus stops and pavements.
Slowly the morning recedes
Behind the tin sheds
Of the city's latest slum.

Road to Nowhere

I see in a dream an earthen cross
On which hang the nameless three:
A wish
A desire
A hopelessness;
Bleeding in the joints and
Fading in blood pools,
Over which they come and erect
The stage for a grand rehearsal,
For an opera in honor
Of a fading life wish.
I wake up to see myself
Still hanging on the cross
Set up at the crossroad
From where the roads lead to nowhere.

Ah! Summer

June.

A stretched lazy afternoon.

Silences keep wailing
Over and over again
In dusty narrow lanes;
A lonely kite in the naked blue sky
Circles over barren mourning roads.
A bunch of urchins benignly
Watch urinating animals
Under the neem tree.
An overfed cockroach crawls
In semicircles on the cracked floor,
Stretching distances in this small room
Over vacant yawns.

A pungent body odour lingers on!

Terrain of Tranquility

Word by word I shrink,
Recede into the night;
Hearing my own voice
Beckoning me from a void
Beyond the distant stars in
The Milky Way.

The telephone bell
Keeps ringing
In the empty, dark room
And reverberates
In rhythmic variations
Over events of busy yesterdays.

A tiny insect flutters
Around the timid glow
Of a lonely lamp post
And finds a haven
On a nameless pavement
In a shanty town.

Silence interprets events
On this waxing night
In variations through many overturns,
And the specs of liquid time
Grow into giants and fairies,
Seeking explanations
From fickle little angels of
Timid nostalgias.

The Carry-Overs

My soliloquies echo
Over the silences,
Symbolize
The wastage of self
Slowly
Over the years.

Bit by bit
The memories tick off,
A haze of sensation
Remains
Over the experiences.

Events linger helplessly
In newsprint till afternoon,
And thereafter,
Get condensed into
Fragments of memories.

Sitting in my ill-lit room
This evening,
I count, recount
The gains, the losses,
Carrying over only things
Unnamed, unexplained.

I Do Not Know

I do not know what to write,
I can't think of anything right.
Foggy mornings, like ghosts of my past,
Hover around, but do not sound
The clarinet of temptations
That played on my senses
Without reminiscences.

There was a night
When my wishes took flight
To unknown lands
Where terrorists ruled,
Firing their guns on half-sleeping kids;
Infants of my desires, they're
Left orphaned now.

Today I know they will not come to me
But will whisper to those ghosts
Who sit in silence once again

In valleys veiled in winter fog;
They will descend to hear my songs
Because soon, very soon,
I will return to my half-burnt attic
Of unfulfilled wishes and orphan desires,
Unknown, unsung, unheard, anonymous!

I Know

A non happening
I know, I think.
But I know that I don't know.
What is there to know after all?
The clockwork universe ticks
And continues life as it were,
Like a web woven by events
And desperate desires crying aloud.

Losing my brand value over the years,
I hang like a parchment on a rusted nail,
Keeping the company of a bored lizard
Hanging clumsily on the crumbling beam.
Do not google me, my friend,
I am neither a name nor a trend.
Like a rusted signboard I am
Hung on a half-broken wall
Near the garbage dump,
Sharing space with pigs and stray dogs.
What do you think I am?

Or I am not?

Whatever way you think,
Think of me
As I too think of myself,
Till the sun settles beyond the tin-roofed shanties
Where too people live
Who think like us,
Or perhaps don't think
Of a non happening in their lives
That is a happening
Always!

Kamathipura

My first thought was a sentiment, the next a look at the self.

Thereafter was an unending flow of verbiage, like

Words pouring out from a computer's memory;

Words that whiz through the sweat pores,

Thoughts that swish like the scorched wind, churned

On a sultry night on a ten by ten strip of pavement

In front of a door in Kamathipura.

"Are your thoughts too personal", "too private" you said.

Sharing them once was enough, when the road was rough,

When there was no place to go to, except

To the solace of a condom-seeking sentiment

With one time use;

Just one time.

The poetry crafted from embalmed words,
With silent metaphors thrown in between,
Lies like a corpse dressed by an undertaker.
"How wonderful!" say the mourners,
Transforming the same into memorable lyrics
To be sung by the latest pop group
Against a glitzy backdrop on MTV.
The poetry lives by a symbol, a brand,
The gadgetry tells it all.

Yes, I was once a poet who bared it all.
But I have stopped existing to myself long ago
Except as my own apparition, still wrapped
In a torn gunny sack on the pavement of
Kamathipura!

* Kamathipura is a red light district in Mumbai.

Ennui

Vacant thoughts yawn nonchalantly on an afternoon
Littered with drafts of poetry and unfinished songs;
Imagination lies dormant, frosted
Under the icicles of Creativity.
Nothing happens.
Nothing seems to happen.
Identities dissolve into fragments of antique wishes,
Abstractions hover around the senses;
A spin of schizophrenia keeps knocking
The doors of a ventriloquist's ambition.
Suddenly the scene dissolves
Into naked apparitions of fairies, elves and gnomes
Drifting in the ruins of an old castle
On the periphery of a dead town called Aspiration.
The grey fangs of air
Keep rocking the empty chair,
A slogan-shouting mob passes by,

Leaving quivering islands of pale crooked light
Shed by brooding lamp posts.
On the far end of a lonely nameless road,
I seek solace in the wilderness of dull sensations
Let loose by the wild cries of desperate silences.

I Was, I Am

I was five feet one when twelve

I am five feet one at fifty-one;

In between was the time

Raping the years till the bones,

Greeting a weird pleasure till

The crimson blood formed into a crust.

In my memories of a conscious manhood of little consequence,

I have known my dear ones grinning through their cavitied mouths

While teaching me the mores of a wasted adulthood

Transfixed like a hymen on a virgin stick on the drainpipe wall.

Yes, they took my childhood for comic appeal

Or at best a figure of compassion for wasted childhood.

My mother, my father and all the dear ones came in a chorus

For pagan celebrations. The altar was my trampled faith;

They took away my smiles for the sacrifice

And left my thoughts bleeding in the night.

How do you consider this an inaugural event for the myth called life?

My life that shared the air of fermented sewage drains and entered

The playfield where a game had just ended in a bloody brawl?

Nothing came to conclusion, nothing terminated in a purpose.

I was in the arena like Spartacus and also in the stalls

Like an intoxicated king cheering the ones about to die.

They said it is all in the game.

Complex?

Weird?

Confused?

Trivial?

Inconsequential?

I am more than all this because I was to be that.

I tried to be different but no, it could not be.

I must also conform to the mould made by my master.

You can interpret an event in a thousand ways

And append a meaning to your own brand,

Lend a thousand dimensions to the subtle smile of Mona Lisa.

I interpreted myself in my own strange way,

But before I could know the fallacies, gauge the irreverence

It was too late, I was fifty-one!

Among friends I feigned respectability;

Among bosses I feigned imbecility.

I talked about my pedigree, moved with a tailcoat,

Ate with a fork, discussed Kafka, dissected Bellow,

Took the dogs for a walk.

A Confession

From that moment on
I could never be
The man of my own intentions.
My senses became the negation of my awareness,
A conscious denial of my motives;
My age hatched a plot
With quivering, naked aspirations,
To make my motives bestsellers in paperbacks.

That was the moment
I bartered my dream
For a spotlight;
Exchanged respectability
With building sales records of
Pep-pills and contraceptives.

Standing at the crossroads
I distributed fragments of memories
As souvenirs to hesitant clients,

And came back home
Metamorphosed
As a caterpillar
Searching the grassroots
Through crawling footsteps.

A Stammering Crow

Did you ever see a stammering crow?

I did once in my nascent days,
When my wishes prepared for flight.
When every night was an Arabian night,
When I could talk aloud with my dreams,
When my whispers were loud as screams.

Walking on a car-choked road, alone
With a bundle of fluorescent desires,
I saw a crow skipping on top of a shed,
Trying to fly, stumbling, trying, stumbling.

Why did my eyes rest on this crow?
The crow looked at me.
Sizing me up, perhaps?
Or sharing his anonymity
With my own namelessness?
I saw it suddenly diving to me

Despite the heavy traffic flow,
Hitting his head on a glass pane;
Tumbling under the car's wheels
He spoke to me in a faltering voice,
He stammered, fluttering his injured wings
Unable to control his life's strings.

I wish I had known the language of crows
To say hello to him at least,
But he gave me no time,
No time to say even Hi!
I saw him crushed under the car's wheels
And I moved on, stumbling
Between the medley of cars
Mumbling between my lips
A faint fumbling sorry,
Just that, nothing more.

The Fade-Out

My wife and I
One night
Exchanged glances
Through silent stances
Around the creaking
Ceiling fan
And made a discovery
That life is
A simple mechanism
Of a smooth fade-out.

Yesterday Always

Washed to the shores of anonymity,
Naked, forlorn, uncared,
I write in the sand
My love poems in italics
And sing to the wayward winds
The song of my dwarfed desires.

I look at the pale blue sky,
And the meandering vastness around,
Something starts hissing below my torso.
Slowly, venom creeps treacherously in the nerves,
Depravity knocks the senses,
And the masochist in me
Tears off the crumbling shreds of memory.
All stands still in the realm of thoughts
Strange shrill sounds echo in the vacuum all around.

The stench of nothingness prevails everywhere,
Nothing happens as nothing had happened before.
My love poems wither away
And the songs fade in the juke box din.
I am the happiest man with no regrets,
I have just seen a day like any other day, roll by,

Behold the Morals

The day wears off beyond the hills,
Wide awake I look into the darkness;
Moons floating on distant skies
Caress me into a dream-loaded sleep.

I don't know whether
It's a Soothsayer's wish
Or a Prophet's prophesy,
Whether it's my ego
Or my chance to go beyond
The coops of seasoned wishes,
Beyond the pretty wonderments
Of skimpy allurements.
But I wish to feel beyond
The gummy summer mornings, and
Resume my journey into nowhere land.

It's no fun, my dear friends
Searching in the dead, pale sky
For purposeful motives
And life's countless errands.

Life, after all, is not a mink coat
Nor is it an antidote
For late night drinking bouts,
Nor is it a matter of opinion
Of mendicants or boy scouts;
Neither is it a plea for politics.
I feel life in my faltered coat
Hanging on a rusted nail,
Dangling in sad silhouettes
Against the walls, naked and pale.

I tally my consciousness with
Cautious footsteps and rationed smiles,
Word by word, I die
Receding into the night,
And hear my own voice echo
Far unto the stars.
The telephone bell rings
Through waves of silence,
Joining the buzz
Of a helpless insect

Fluttering around the lipstick stain
On my wrinkled pillow.

Suddenly the hearse halts
At my doorstep,
And they carry from it
A silver painted coffin
With my name inscribed in gold;
Silently I step into the coffin
Without protest,
Awaiting my moment of fading
In a pyramid of unrealized ambitions.

Life, an Anti-life

My friends, well-wishers, dear ones!
Count me out of your world;
Count me in when the clock turns back.

You may make dreams
And keep them safe in glass domes,
Create your icons,
The fairies, elves and gnomes.
But I can't keep a dream
Captive in my wishes' screams.
Nor can I bind a memory
With a rubber band;
I also cannot understand
The peeling of sentiments
Like dried onions,
Looking with awe
At my own predicaments.
My friends, my well-wishers, dear ones!
Don't treat nights as dream-making apparatus,

Nor the days as dormant specs
Of a forgotten past.

With a life half-spun
It's no fun, dear friends!
Searching in rough hewn skies
Brand value for life's trends.
Life, after all, is not a pictured frame
Or a national hero's name.
It's neither a matter of opinion
Of Hegel, Kant or Kierkegaard
Nor is it a forum for a reunion
Of old war veterans.

All that happens around is an assumption
Of nothingness.

An Explanation

Tranquility!
A cup of hot coffee
After a sleepless night
With an old prostitute.

Peace!
Seeing a crime thriller
With the wife
After a heated argument.

Love!
Postscript of memories
Revised repeatedly
On marriage anniversaries.

Prosperity!
A stack of empty tins
Stored for stocktaking
For posterity.

A mothball of definitions?

A Dark Cold Night

Slowly the stars rise and night appears
Swinging back and forth,
Filling the room with benign compassion,
Where they all sit for old time's sake,
The men holding their whiskies between half smiles,
Occupied silences, wishing for an early moonshine.

Slowly the shadows shrink to the fringes of the silk tapestry,
Reminding them of the days of grandpas
Who left the world
Choked with arthritis and cold memories.
The night etches realities on dark silhouettes,
Holding their pulse and feeling their hearts.
Most of what they intentioned remained undone,
And what they did turned acid and soil.

Slowly their gazes get fixed,
Thoughts become cold,

As my grandpa found many times
Happening to him, when he sat
Smoking his pipe on the huge couch
On dark cold nights like this.

Past midnight, the moon rises in midair,
The night stops hissing,
Winds cease rocking,
The shadows stand still.
Something happens to them,
Those ladies and gentlemen.
They rise in their chairs,
Steadying their footsteps
In the midst of fading memories,
And moth-eaten thoughts—
Suddenly file past, moist-eyed, silent,
Waving their half-raised hands to
This dark cold night.

An Ode to Our Times

Day and Night—two dwarfs
Dance on the hump of hallucinations
To the beat of weary hopes.

A culture expresses itself—
Kling-klang, klik-klak, caw-caw
Whir-whir, whiz-whiz, ooh-ah-aw—
And vanishes in the mascara-thickened
Listless eyes of a tired call girl.

Blood keeps oozing from the nerves
On narrow staircases in back lanes,
Clotting on the footpaths;
Licked by stray, rabid dogs.

Flies keep licking sweat
From damp brows,
Leaving their eggs to incubate
In the dark cavities of the brain.

Naked corpses of sentiments decompose
On bright neon lamps,
Bearing a gesture of goodwill
Towards affluent buyers.

Old grandpas ogle at each other,
Laughing through their hollow cheekbones,
Counting the gains of survival
In torn pockets of their soiled pants.

Autumn Leaves

Autumn is here today,
Autumn will be here tomorrow,
Autumn will be always, may be.

I don't know where other seasons have gone,
Why the morning birds are silent,
Why the butterflies have stopped their dance,
Why the baby sun has stopped its romance
With my half-closed window; neither do I know
Why silences mourn like hapless widows.

Across the dusty window panes
I see a pile of yellow leaves
Littered on the pavement;
And a pale blue sky beyond
Helpless and silent naked trees.

I stumbled on a heap of these leaves
One evening,
And the half moon mocked,
The naked trees rocked,

The naughty winds laughed;
"This is what you are?
You, the son of man,
Anonymous, diminishing, decaying
Like these helpless autumn leaves."

Stretched on my armchair this evening
I see only this eternal pile
Of twisted, curled, yellow leaves
Day after day,
Always.
Bathed in the pale silhouette
Of a stained half moon
Wishing for a fade-out,
Slowly, silently.

A Loveless Night

The winds are going astray,
The dust from by lanes,
Enters the brain.
Through the attic the moon peeps,
Outside my door a dog weeps.
Bizarre thoughts,
Disheveled feelings,
Listless mornings,
Vacant evenings,
Beckon like sleepy whores
After a loveless night
Once again.

A Moonless Night

Then I spoke.

Spoke of a moonless night,
Frigid, morbid, transient, loose,
Stretched from nowhere to nowhere.
The sounds set to motion the moonless night
On hisses of sulking vultures,
Perched on decadent boughs of aged trees.

The winds work overtime, over fatigued senses,
Working with a surgeon's scalpel, incisive and calm.
Deep in the spine's marrow
Something oozes out and
Mingles in the darkness
As quickly as the silence works over torments
Of a lonely traveler, waylaid in endless ravines
Of a time which never stands still. Never!

Countless

Countless are the nightmares
I have done to death.
Some with the H-bomb of Time;
The man, indestructible,
Why not?
More ancient
Than Matsya.

Two instant poets—
One sensitive
Raised to the power of infinity,
The other
As sensitive as a steel bloom,
And as grey
As the Arabian Sea
Looking like a loving and
Unwashed grandfather.

The Smile
Of the flower child
Like infant Lord Krishna
Presenting thirty-three crore Gods
In his utterly butterly mouth;
The whole encounter
Was like meeting Dali
In good old Vrindavan,
With all of Dali's subjects
Alive
Pulsating.

Night Shift

The sounds are the same, so are the sentiments,
The world a mess of dark grey skyline to skyline.
Under the mercury vapor, dull and dazed
Like an urchin grown old
On the city's pavements,
Lazy sensations keep rhythm with machines,
Retreating instinctively when clocks strike midnight.
A patch of dreams glued to heavy eyelids
Tries to join the barking dogs
Hovering outside the factory gates;
The fluttering calendar on a sooty wall
Announces the date that has just slipped by.

Time stacked in a Tiffin box
Reveals itself in yawns and weary desires,
And gets transfixed again
On the thumping thuds beyond tall flames.
Thoughts stage a grand rehearsal
In the ante-chamber of weak memories,
Wishing to go back home where they
All slumber, perched on tomorrow's dreams.

Om Shri Ganeshayah Namah!

First the invocation and then the grand drama!
Actors with paint and grease,
Smelling of tobacco and odorous sweat,
Appear in the midst of whistles and cat calls.
That is not all.

Spirits are aroused as the leader appears
Onstage to make the announcement—
All that's happening is for his efforts—
As he is the one who ferrets
All that is good and desirable in our lofty tradition,
Always presented with such boisterous rendition,
With gusto and aplomb
With sentiment and song,
With dancers amidst din and roar.

Urchins registering excitement with piss, giggle
And ribaldry; women eyeing the favorite players,
Drooling with desire, dreams and disdain,
Rubbing their eyes of kohl, sleep and lewd
thoughts

Sighing for a gentle rub with one who plays Harishchandra.

The one who sells *chana* by day transforms into a

Character divine under gaslights and looks so bright,

Smooth as a lemon peel, no, like the betel nut

Which he chews with a heroic gut even when he emotes a sob.

The show goes on till the king and the king's men
Witness the crimson apparition in the distant skies
And the leader gives a yawn to signal the stop
Which they do not desire; the urchins,
The menfolk and ladies, desiring the next
Night for honing their sentiments and a wish to
Return to a world which does not belong to them!

Once Upon a Time

Once upon a time
When birds sang and nature chimed,
When jasmine buds were not laced
With gunpowder,
The way to my village was kissed
By mango blossoms, and
The old peepal tree told stories
Of times gone by;
Once upon a time
When the single small boat
Floating on the naughty stream,
Pointed to the flock of geese
Flying from nowhere to nowhere
To touch the sky's log beam;
Once upon a time
When I was young and
Often strayed into alleys
Of sheer thoughtlessness
Looking at the distant horizon,

Logistics of Progress

A wish echoes:
Wish!
Wish!!
Wish!!!

Consciousness expands:
Triangles,
Squares,
Rectangles

Signature of destiny
(on dotted lines)
Animations
Privations
Isolations

Rationale of ethics:

Go

Stop

Go

Way to progress:

An unwritten agreement

Between

The genius and a synthetic gene.

Morning at Puri Beach

Silences moan o'er the sea,
The violent waves
Kiss the winds and come back
O'er the waves again.

The sky turns a shade
Of deep crimson
And melts into gold, lazing
O'er and o'er the waves again.

Ripple after ripple spreads
O'er the flutter of seabirds
Half dazed, half rhapsodized,
On and on and on....

Hesitant and timid light specs
Reveal a relevance
To dimpled grey sands
Washed by the waves again and again.

The fishermen cast their nets
Far and wide, o'er
Their own silhouettes
In the mid horizon.

A blushing baby sun blinks
In the lap of the frigid, naked morning.
This moment never fades.
O'er the waves again.
Never.

Rain

Today again the rain came.
The way it never came before.

I have heard the rain song all through my years.
Heard the torrent, felt the sweeping wind,
Saw the drops slip through bending twigs.
But that was all to the rains
As it has been to all Decembers; they came
Like crooked compulsions of a self-obsessed time machine.

Today when the rain came, the fury was absent
There was no break dance.
I gazed at the sky and saw the meandering formations
Of clouds fly by in silent procession, as they
Took those boys away to the trembling street corner
For a quick execution.

The thunder of the gunpowder and the sulphur fumes
Bore the only testimony of this silent rain.
I was not there to wipe the tiny sweat beads
Which mingled with the grime and sultry June
And became history to reverberate
Through all oncoming rains through the ages.

A Phantom Fantasy

What was it that crossed my way
On a rain-soaked night when I walked alone;
When winds roared and the shroud of clouds
Covered the helpless night;
When silence, mingled with the violins of raindrops,
Sang in a soprano, shrill and loud?

I saw you emerging from quivering shadows
Apparition-like,
Rising above puddles of stagnant water
On the cracked road.
You were smiling, I saw, like Mona Lisa,
Or Saraswati in a Ravi Varma calendar,
Or a sexy siren in a movie poster.

Was it really you or was it a happening
In the dark chamber of my somnolent wishes,
When I wished you to appear on a moonlit night

On the dusky shores of a nameless lake
Beyond the horizon, sky walking with me?
You and me, me and you
Hand in hand, on the streetcar of clouds
Surfing the winds, slowly descending
To soak ourselves in each other's essence.

But what I saw
Were the dark evening shadows
Dancing to the tune of roaring winds.
I helplessly walked towards my shanty,
To sleep in my five by four room with a leaky roof
To wake up again for the next morning shift!

A Happening

It happens sometimes that we are strangers,
Treating memories as mere passersby,
Trying to discover each other anew
On a still grey night in a distant caravan serai.
Probing thoughts, exchanging silences
In the faltering glow of a small wicker lamp,
Touching each other with opaque glances,
Reckoning the chances of a breakthrough
That comes haltingly through
Taciturn smiles on hazy profiles.
Sentiments rushing with gongs and drums
Desires winking through half-closed eyes,
Slowly, with packed nostalgias in memory bags
We start our journey again, afresh,
Still strangers, trying to discover each other anew.

We, On a Hill Road

On that winding road
We were sweat and smell,
Whispering to the wayward clouds,
Calling the hills and trees aloud;
Fading in depths of endless abstractions,
Riding again on the lump of wishes.
All the way, we thought
Of winds, talked of springs
Touched silences,
Tended the patchy sunshine
With meaningful glances.
Up and down
Our shadows kept pace
With wondering astonishment,
Handing over the incidents
To brooding trees, meandering rivulets,
Silent hills and whispering meadows.
A narrow strip of sky
Became our ally
Before we discovered
Our complete strangeness
With each other.

A Feeling

The happenings mingle with desires
And fly to the sky where stars stage a concert;
The moon, the winds, the clouds come with a fanfare
Over the way that passes through the valley of ecstasy,
And come to rest where earth meets the sky
Over a crimson horizon and sit for a ritual wet with a happening.
Slowly a smile descends;
The waves in two fluid eyes rise with a rhythm
The hearts pulsate and wishes terminate on a feeling that is you!

This Winter Day!

This winter day,
In the lazy sunshine
Birds hesitate to spread wings;
Thoughts shivering, limbs quivering
Along on the terrace
I see the vapors of my breath
Taking the form of goblins.
Garbled wishes
Rolling on quivering thoughts,
Doodle the outline of the crimson bra
I saw peeping
From your dress,
When we met on
That misty December night
Under the stars
With a timid moon
As our witness.
Under the gaze of a hazy sun this day
I don't have any witness

Of my unsaid intentions,
I just assume the outlines
Of those obstructions
Taking the form
Of a surreal painting
Over my misty breath,
And try to weave a tapestry of
You in my mind
Alone, on my terrace
On this cold winter day.

One December Morning

This shaky silent Morning
Is the bruised face of Night
Tortured to desperation
By naked frigidity.
Hesitant and reluctant,
She steps out slowly through the veiled mist,
Hiding her anguish behind a pale sky.
And asks the dew-soaked leaves in whispers,
The whereabouts of her father
By all called Day.

Tomorrow I

Let's live this night
In bits and fragments,
And bury the long long day
Under the ageing trees
Which shed their leaves
In aimless disdain.
Let's, for a while, not understand
What the senses cannot comprehend.

We know things are hopelessly bad
The plight of man is really sad:
Prices are rising;
Economy's bad;
Promises are hollow;
Intentions are fake;
The leaders perched on rooftops shout
But man is still a church mouse.

Let's share this night
With tea and moonshine,
As again, tomorrow
May not be ours.

Tomorrow II

The day ends
When talks terminate;
The weary thoughts struggle
For a purpose for tomorrow,
And the day after, and the day beyond
Till the incidents freeze into fossils,
And we keep memories
In our cupboards with mothballs.
Our wishes and volitions
Wake with the time clock,
When we rise to depart
With promises in our hearts
For a future reunion,
Perhaps tomorrow, or the day after,
Or the day beyond.

Tomorrow III

Today is a dead day
Like a rotten fish thrown away.

I do not know what she meant
When grandma pushed a plate
Of sago, milk and honey
Before the tomcat,
And kept telling the stories
Of bygone days, of noble kings
And their spoilt brats.
Evoking a sense of despair, on contemporariness perhaps
In toothless smiles and benign overtures;
Looking at the vacant sky and sighing aloud,
Wishing this day a quick repose,
Hoping perhaps something may happen tomorrow.

Tomorrow IV

I am in a narrow lane
Watching the dust-smeared urchins
Urinating on pavements with gay abandon.

It is the time when elders
Chant their morning prayers
And leave for work in their working flairs.

I see the shadows grow
And twist on the walls,
The minds engulfing the empty street malls.

The urchins gather under a banyan tree,
Filling the void with shrieks and scornful howls
And emptying their bowels
In the field of slush.

Soon the night will descend
And the urchins will huddle around
In the cursed fairyland of their pavement dwellings.
This day will thus wear out
To make a start again
Tomorrow.

Victory Parade

When I wrote those poems
I had the smell of lilies
In my nostrils,
I wrote those lines
In honor of a feasty dream.

I saw the moon melt
On a fluid night
Dripping in ringlets on
Many minor wishes; and
Imagination weaving patterns of
Soft cloud flakes
On the wings
Of a high-flying bird.

I did not know the name of the bird
As all the birds those days
Soared high in the deep blue sky;
I wrote those poems to commemorate
A wish fulfillment.

The words sometimes flutter like butterflies
In the midst of a turbulent storm
And snoop down on the
Tormented anguish of a soldier's widow.

An orphan child keeps fiddling
With wax images of gods and godlings,
The silence spreads like the anguish
Of a raped teenager.
What do I do?
I don't know.

An orphan child, keeps nibbling
The waxen faces of baby angels.
Only a few of the war veterans
March in formations
On the barren streets,
Holding their pennants across their shoulders,
Proclaiming to themselves, the victory of
An alien death wish.

I stretch my words
Over tattered fragments
Of sentiments
Tacking them over the canvas
Of frigid faiths.

My intentions ogle at me
Like an old prisoner on parole
Viewing environs with strange bewilderment
Through the lens of a bygone past.

I divide my strangeness among my partners
Of yesteryears and fractured boyhood,
But I cannot console them with
Just a motive, a brittle sympathy or
Somnolent sentiments.

Wait

Deep within
A pang, an itch,
A persistent thought
An incident;
Or just a thought
A rumble from the past, perhaps,
Whatever, whatever...
The moon hanging on a cliff, lonely
Like me, seeking something
I don't know what,
An abstraction, perhaps,
A wish hanging on the doorknob
For you to return.
The empty corridors, the rusted doors,
Empty windows mocking the moon
Return to my mind's dark cell
Of a fake dream.

I scream.
Draculas of silence
Suck the white corpuscles
Of my abstract thoughts.
Nothingness can be a boon
If I compromise with the abstraction within,
Causing pain that constantly penetrates
The warm naked pores of my existence
When I look around for you!

Walk

Walk till the road's end
Walk till the last river bend
Picking the specs of time
As the winds touch hair and chime.
Walk with wet feet
Where the morning sun meets
The lazy truckers' fleet.
Standing at the crossroads, see the fun
Of psychedelic fumes teasing the sun.
You are not the nation of one
Like the Moon, the Pole Star, the Sun,
Walk along the crowd, the urchins and the old,
Meandering your way through the ancient roads.
Walk, walk, walk till the road's end,
Walk, dear friend, till the last river bend.

Yesterday Always

Washed to the shores of anonymity,
Naked, forlorn, uncared,
I write in the sand
My love poems in italics
And sing to the wayward winds
The song of my dwarfed desires.

I look at the pale blue sky,
And the meandering vastness around,
Something starts hissing below my torso.
Slowly, venom creeps treacherously in the nerves
Depravity knocks the senses,
And the masochist in me
Tears off the crumbling shreds of memory,
All stands still in the realm of thoughts
Strange shrill sounds echo in the vacuum all around.

The stench of nothingness prevails everywhere,
Nothing happens as nothing had happened before.
My love poems wither away
And the songs fade in the juke box din.
I am the happiest man with no regrets,
I have just seen a day like any other day, roll by.

You

Were you working till late in the night?
Your messages came with a yawny plight
I was awake 'coz the wind and the storm
Kept pounding on my doorless dorm.
Yahoo! said you were awake.
Or was it a happening fake?
Was it duty's call
Or was it a wish's recall?
I read your messages and sat back
On my crooked old chair
To look and stare
At the gathering clouds
Deep in the sky
Coming to kiss my somnolent desires.
Perhaps this was my wish,
If not, then why do I soak my pores
In the thunder and deafening roars.
Let the rains wet my bones
And soften the hard rocky stones;
Let my eyes be awake
To read in rhythm your messages
Tonight, once again

As I did every night
To wish for your smile
On the distant horizon of my desires,
Thinking when the rains smile
You will, for once,
Will call me back through your messages
For a while!